Picasso's Artful Occupation

by Ian Buckley

Published by Playdead Press 2014

© Ian Buckley 2014

Ian Buckley has asserted his rights under the Copyright, Design and Patents Act, 1988, to be identified as the author of this work.

A CIP catalogue record for this book is available from the British Library.

ISBN 978-1-910067-08-6

Caution
All rights whatsoever in this play are strictly reserved and application for performance should be sought through the author before rehearsals begin. No performance may be given unless a license has been obtained.

This book is sold subject to the condition that it shall not by way of trade or otherwise, be lent, resold, hired out, or otherwise circulated without the publisher's prior consent in any form of binding or cover other than that in which it is published and without a similar condition including this condition being imposed on the subsequent purchaser.

Playdead Press
www.playdeadpress.com

Picasso's Artful Occupation was first produced at The Baron's Court Theatre, London, in March 2014, with the following cast:

Pablo Picasso   Gary Heron

Willi Frisch   Roberto Landi

Franz Hebbel   David O'Connor

Directed by Kenneth Michaels
Designed by Cleo Harris-Seaton
Lighting and stage management by Phoebe Salter

Ian Buckley
Picasso's Artful Occupation

'I was brought up in a communist family, and the fact that Picasso joined the French Communist party six weeks after the end of the Second World War, and remained in it for the rest of his life, gave me a particular interest in this most wonderful and iconoclastic of artists. It was a short step from there to wondering how he lived his life under the Nazi occupation. For five long years, 1940 to 1945, he lived and worked in Paris, forbidden to exhibit his Bolshevik-degenerate art to the public.

How did he, the best-known artist alive, deal with a capricious and all-powerful German regime? What choices did he make? Was he protected by sympathetic members of the occupying regime or did he survive by luck, cunning and discretion?

In my play set in the shady vaults of a Paris bank where Picasso has been summoned for the grand inventory of his works, I hope I'm able to give some 'answers' to these questions. The play is based on an actual historical event.'

Ian went to Christ's College Cambridge from the Elliott Comprehensive in Putney and, having obtained an Honours degree in English Literature and a soccer blue, he then gained an MA from The University of Kent, researching the works of Sean O'Casey. Then it was time to change course.

Be creative not critical. Be a playwright. That's what he's been doing ever since.

Ian has had a number of plays performed on the London fringe: *The Tailors' Last Stand* (Baron's Court Theatre); *Keeping Faith* (The King's Head); *First Timers* (The Duke's Head); *Suits and Blouses* (The Room at The Orange Tree); *Down The River* (Theatre Royal, Stratford East, touring show); *Tainted Love* (The Young Actors' Theatre).

He's been shortlisted for the following playwriting competitions: the Verity Bargate Award; the Maddermarket Award; The Bruntwood Manchester Royal Exchange (long shortlisted with *The Return*); the Brockley Jack 'Write Now Three' competition.

He's had a play on BBC Radio Four, *Changing Gear*, re-broadcast in translation on Hessische Rundfunk in Germany, who also broadcast *The Revolutionary*.

The rumour that he's made any money from his pen is entirely unfounded.

Characters

Pablo PICASSO
59 – the most famous artist in the world; charismatic, intelligent, worried

Officer Willi FRISCH
25 – low-ranking officer in German Army of Occupation; sensitive, artistic, probably gay, admires Picasso

Officer Franz HEBBEL
26 – same grade officer; a rogue, out for the main chance, cunning and untrustworthy

The events take place in occupied Paris in 1940, in the vaults of the Banque Nationale pour le Commerce et l'Industrie, shortly after the Armistice between France and Germany.

Stage in darkness: we hear footsteps echo down a corridor

Hebbel   How much further?

Picasso   We're here.

We hear a light being switched on

A dim light lights up the stage. We can make out an underground vault

A large iron door is unlocked

The door creaks open

The audience begins to dimly make out a crazy mountain of paintings

Three men enter the vault. Hebbel and Frisch in German army uniform, Picasso in a loose-fitting, good quality overcoat

It's been raining heavily outside. The men's coats are soaking

Frisch takes his greatcoat off and shakes wet off it, folds it neatly and places it by gate. Hebbel undoes his and knocks a bit of the wet off. Picasso ignores any wet on his

Hebbel lets out a whistle as he looks round

Hebbel   My god!

Frisch	There's mountains of it!
Hebbel	Talk about pile 'em high.

Hebbel puts hand on a level of paintings. The whole pile moves dangerously

Hebbel	This all yours?
Picasso	It is.
Frisch	You must paint in your sleep!
Picasso	I assure you I'm always awake when I paint.
Hebbel	Why're they dumped here like this?
Picasso	Well I don't know about...
Frisch	Like so much junk.
Picasso	I can't sell them. The market's dead!
Hebbel	Hah! Listen to him. Another artist who can't make ends meet! We see lots of them, don't we, Frisch?
Frisch	I don't know about...

Hebbel	They're the only sort we EVER see. One day we're going to meet an artist who makes a good living...
Frisch	Maybe Herr Picasso doesn't want to sell his paintings.
Hebbel	Yeah what... suits him to hide them away.
Picasso	Why would I want to hide my paintings away?
Hebbel	Hold them back - push up the price.
Frisch	The law of supply and demand.
Picasso	If only! With my paintings it's less supply less demand!
Hebbel	Why not increase the supply?
Picasso	The galleries are all shut.

Frisch wipes dust off a frame with finger, ostentatiously

Frisch	(*Looking at dust on finger*) They've been shut this long?
Hebbel	...We believe you Monsieur Picasso. Money's tight for you artists. We know that

	big car you get chauffeur-driven round in runs on air. Well... shall we start?
Picasso	Can you go through it again... I didn't understand.
Frisch	We're listing your works.
Picasso	Listing them how?
Hebbel	Well um... what they're made of...
Picasso	I told you - canvas and paint...
Frisch	Date painted.
Picasso	Some of them took years.
Frisch	The finish date will do.
Picasso	And this is in aid of what?
Hebbel	Um... your protection Herr Picasso. If anyone wants to nick your stuff... sell it... we can check... it's down here in black and white.
Picasso	It's to help me?
Frisch	To help us to help you.

Hebbel	If you ever need it.
Picasso	...I'll have to guess dates. I don't keep a diary.
Hebbel	A guess will be fine.
Frisch	We'll need a title for each work.
Hebbel	And whether there's any jewels stashed in the frames hahaha!
Frisch	The paintings are the jewels in the frame I think Herr Picasso would say.
Picasso	So the date painted, materials used...?
Hebbel	And very important - how much they're worth - if a poor artist like you was lucky enough to sell one of them that is. Right, shall we start?
Frisch	If I pull this one out, we'll work to the right.

We see Frisch tug at a painting to use as a starting place. Picasso watches anxiously

Hebbel joins in the tugging with Frisch

The pile of paintings creaks ominously

Picasso	STOP! DON'T TOUCH! YOU'LL PULL THE WHOLE BLOODY LOT DOWN!

Hebbel and Frisch stop. In doing so Frisch catches his hand and cuts it on a sharp piece of frame

Frisch	Scheisse! My hand! (*Sucks cut*)
Hebbel	We don't normally get bellowed at like that, do we Frisch. Very rare.
Picasso	No it's just… have you handled paintings before?
Hebbel	I've moved 'em about.
Picasso	Professionally I mean. In a gallery?
Hebbel	Not me I'm afraid.
Frisch	Once or twice.
Picasso	Then can I do it? Move my paintings? If you don't mind, I mean.
Hebbel	Well I… can't say it'd bother me.
Frisch	I don't mind.
Hebbel	Ready, steady, go, then Monsieur Picasso.

Picasso painstakingly pulls out a painting. He puffs and pants spectacularly

Hebbel   Heave ho! And out!

Painting comes out

Hebbel takes a folding wooden ruler from his pocket, extends it, measures painting

Picasso   Sorry to keep on but can you measure on the back? On the front might scratch the work.

Hebbel   Absolutely! I left my brain at home - what I've got of one. (*He laughs*)

Hebbel measures the first painting, on the back, with his ruler

     50 by 49! Get it down Frisch!

Frisch   50... by... 49.

Picasso   Oil on canvas... 1910.

Hebbel   Title?

Picasso   Flat Fish on Wet Plate.

Hebbel   What would it sell for?

Picasso	...It's not for sale.
Hebbel	Say you did sell it - what would it fetch?
Picasso	I really can't with this one. It's for my personal collection.
Hebbel	Come on - every painting has its price.
Picasso	Not this. It has memories.
Hebbel	Forty thousand francs... at least.
Picasso	Are you a dealer, monsieur? You sound so confident.
Hebbel	I wish I was. Reckon I'd have a bit more to splash around than my measly soldier's pay.
Picasso	I don't think you would. Times are tough for everybody.
Hebbel	Just tell us what it's worth.
Picasso	If I was selling it - and I'm not - twenty thousand francs max.
Hebbel	For a painting by the most famous artist in the world!

Frisch	Seems to me like you're undervaluing.
Hebbel	I could sell a painting of mine for twenty thou' - and I don't paint!
Picasso	Monsieur, please, try. Paint something - I'll lend you brushes and a canvas. If you sell it for twenty thousand - or even half that - it'll be beginner's luck.
Frisch	I bet you'd get twenty five thousand francs for that.
Picasso	Twenty one thousand then. And not a franc more.
Hebbel	Note it Frisch! (*Frisch murmurs as he writes*) We can't under-price! They'll check - our experts. If they think we have, we'll be back to start again and that's a waste of everyone's time. Next.

Picasso replaces painting. It screeches as he pushes it in between two others

He immediately starts pulling out next painting

Picasso	Out...you come!

Hebbel looks at the painting – it's of two women – 'monumental' style

Hebbel	Jesus, I wouldn't fancy getting under her. Be like making love to a steam-roller. Splat over the bed!
Picasso	She's an archetype.
Hebbel	Is that a person who's big all over?
Picasso	The critics said she was ugly. Monsieur Picasso painting rubbish.
Frisch	I like her.
Picasso	Do you Herr Frisch?
Frisch	Well I... yes... I think she's...

Picasso turns painting round. Hebbel measures

Hebbel	Title?
Picasso	Naked Running Woman.
Frisch	(*as he writes*) Naked... Run...
Hebbel	110 by 67. Price?

Picasso	Eighteen thousand... at a pinch.
Hebbel	Twenty two thou' minimum!

Picasso is already pulling out another painting

Picasso	Out my beauty, out... you... come.

Hebbel and Frisch look at it

Hebbel	Well that's more like it - a bullfight!
Frisch	I don't see a matador.
Hebbel	Maybe the bull's eaten him?
Picasso	Actually it's a bull fighting a horse.
Hebbel	Poor horse isn't doing too well, is he? Bull's got its horns through its belly!
Picasso	In this painting the bull wins.
Hebbel	You ever painted one where the horse wins?
Picasso	The horse has its dying glory. That's a victory of sorts.
Hebbel	(*He measures it*) Title?

Picasso   Naughty Bull with Nice Horse.

Hebbel marks each finished painting with a chalk-mark on back

Hebbel   The wife and me've got a painting of a horse. Hanging in our parlour. Kaiser Wilhelm in the saddle. The horse looks like a horse, and the Kaiser looks like a horse and idiots like me can understand it…

Frisch   Are you insulting the Kaiser?

Hebbel   The horse is a cracker! She's got beautiful legs and eyelashes to die for, so where's the insult? 56 by 48! Price?

Picasso   Fifteen thousand on a good day.

Frisch   Too low.

Picasso   Alright sixteen thousand but I doubt you'll get it.

Hebbel   Sixteen it is.

Picasso   (*Pulling out picture*) 'Old Torn Up Newspapers'.

Hebbel   (*Measures*) 60 by 30.

Picasso	(*Pulls out another*) 'Guitar With Bits'.
Hebbel	(*Measuring*) 33 by 20.
Frisch	(*Speaking aloud as he writes*) 'Torn Up... did you say?

A painting moves of its own accord

Picasso	(*As painting moves*) On no! Oh the bastards!
Hebbel	Who? What's the matter?
Picasso	The rats! They've chewed my painting! Seems my cat doesn't scare off rats.
Hebbel	Bloody rodents eh. No respect for art! Title?
Picasso	'The Chewer Chewed', and more rat poison.
Frisch	I'm sorry? What was that?
Picasso	...Up to where?
Frisch	I thought you said 'With Bits'?
Picasso	That was the one before!
Frisch	The one before what?

Picasso	'Chewed'! There's 'Guitar With Bits' and there's 'The Chewer Chewed'.
Frisch	Where does 'Rat Poison' come in?
Picasso	I need to lay some down. Toute suite. To kill them before they make a ratty meal of all my works.
Frisch	I'm sorry I'm miles behind.
Hebbel	Price?
Frisch	No really I'm lost. You'll have to go back a few.
Picasso	...Nineteen thousand francs if everything was in my favour. Otherwise fifteen thousand six hundred.
Hebbel	You're not serious?
Picasso	I am.
Frisch	What came after 'Old Torn Up Newspapers'?
Hebbel	...Be realistic!
Picasso	D'you know the market here in Paris?

Hebbel	I know it more than a bit.
Picasso	So if you know, tell me - what sells? What will people pay money for?

Hebbel no idea

Hebbel	Well um... the Impressionists?
Picasso	Herr Frisch?
Frisch	The Pointillists? Gouachists? (*Picasso nods no*) ...Surrealists... cubists... modernists...? (*Picasso nods no*) ...Primitivists ...new realists?
Picasso	I'll tell you what sells! Photos! You know, 'smile please', point and pop! I don't know why artists don't smash their palettes up and buy cameras - that's what the public wants! So, I've given you a price based on this cultural fact — the ferocious competition from the photo. It's low but it's realistic.
Frisch	I'm sure I've got these wrong. What came after the 'Torn Up Newspapers'?
Picasso	'Guitar With Bits', wasn't it?

Frisch   Did I have a price?

Picasso   Ten thousand on a warm sunny day with a very rich and very generous art-lover.

Picasso pulls out another painting. Lots of grunts with the effort. Frisch noting title

Frisch   That's touching. The way they're holding each other.

Picasso   They're in love.

Hebbel   Why're their feet so big? Have they got a disease?

Picasso   Only in being different.

Frisch   I can see this painting displayed in galleries in Germany.

Hebbel   Their feet would stick out.

Frisch   I'm not looking at their feet!

Hebbel   You don't have to. They hit you in the eye.

Frisch   The only reason you might have for painting these wonderful young people more in proportion, monsieur, would be to

	win over people who were ignorant about art.
Picasso	In proportion how?
Hebbel	He means smaller feet and bigger tits, don't you Willi...
Frisch	No I don't.
Hebbel	Yes you do.
Frisch	You've got no idea about art have you Franz.
Hebbel	You've got no idea about women.
Frisch	I've got as much idea as you.
Hebbel	When you're ready, Monsieur Picasso.
Frisch	What d'you mean by that remark anyway?
Hebbel	Nothing...
Frisch	Tell me or so help me I'll...
Hebbel	You'll what?
Frisch	I think you know what.

Hebbel	Alright, keep your hair on. It was a joke for god's sake.
Frisch	I'm waiting.
Hebbel	All I meant was you don't exactly get on with women.
Frisch	Says who?
Hebbel	...The women I try to fix you up with.
Frisch	They're not my type!
Hebbel	Um... the blokes... in the unit.
Frisch	Because I don't crack jokes about the size of their tits!
Hebbel	Which most men do.
Frisch	Shame on them then, if they can't raise their sights above the end of their penises!
Hebbel	Shame on men who raise theirs to forbidden fruits.
Frisch	I don't know what you're talking about Franz but you'd... well you'd better watch

	yourself. I like women as much as the next man.
Hebbel	So what sort of women do you like Willi?
Frisch	Well... I... athletic women...
Hebbel	I'd shag an athlete any day.
Frisch	You have to lower everything to sex don't you.
Hebbel	You were thinking of running a race talking politics and art were you?
Frisch	...Have you been to Germany, Mr Picasso?
Picasso	I'm awaiting my first invite.
Frisch	You get posters on every street! Young people staring proudly into the distance.
Hebbel	Yeah...lots of people staring proudly into the distance in Germany. None of them have spots or beer bellies...
Frisch	That's because it's the job of the artist to show us how we CAN be. Not how we are.
Hebbel	Who says?

Frisch	Anyone who knows the slightest thing about painting and its power to move and inspire... (*He stops*)

Picasso works a new picture out of its row. He is very aware of the bickering between Frisch and Hebbel

Hebbel	Willi used to paint, didn't you? Back in the old days.
Frisch	We're talking about art, not me.
Hebbel	Young men I believe.
Frisch	Can we get on with the job?
Hebbel	I know because we come from the same town, don't we Willi? Same gymnasium even. He was the best artist by a mile. Loved painting men, didn't you. Young men... in swimming trunks...?
Frisch	Artists often draw the human body, don't they Monsieur Picasso?
Picasso	The human body is central.
Hebbel	I thought it was women men drew.

Picasso	I concentrate on women myself. They excite me more.
Hebbel	Maybe you draw the occasional man?
Picasso	Not often.
Frisch	What does it matter if it's a man or a woman?
Picasso	It matters a lot to me because it's what inspires me. Women always have.
Hebbel	There Willi. Now you've been told. Monsieur Picasso is inspired by women. And you, it would seem, by men.
Frisch	Every artist is different. I'm sure Monsieur will agree with that.
Hebbel	D'you think an artist should stand by his work, Monsieur Picasso? That he's done in the past?
Frisch	So you can make him look a fool every day?
Hebbel	You make me look a fool often enough - making out I'm ignorant about art.

Frisch	I hardly think you qualify as an expert Franz.
Picasso	D'you still draw, Monsieur Frisch?
Frisch	I don't have time.
Picasso	That's a shame... when someone starts and then stops.
Hebbel	Hasn't for months, have you, Willi. Got rid of everything. Destroyed the lot. Poof! On our first leave home, wasn't it, Willi? (*Clicks fingers*) All that art. Up in a cloud of smoke. Don't you think that's a pity, Monsieur Picasso?
Frisch	It's nothing to do with Monsieur Picasso.
Hebbel	I just wondered what he thought...
Frisch	For god's sake can we get on! We've been here ages and we've hardly started!
Picasso	Don't you want monsieur to say?
Frisch	It's not that I don't want him to...
Hebbel	You can't be bothered to hear what a great artist has to say?

Frisch	Can we speed up! All this silly chat, we'll never get finished.
Hebbel	Don't look at me. I'm waiting for a title for this lovely work. (*Moves back to painting*)
Picasso	'The Lovers'.
Hebbel	Price?
Picasso	Twelve thousand one hundred and fifty.

Picasso tries to push the painting back into a gap it doesn't want to go into

	Get in there, sod you!
Hebbel	Noted Willi?
Frisch	I... liked that painting.
Hebbel	No time for chat - we have to speed up.
Frisch	...It's difficult to make suggestions... to a famous artist. Their feet... I'm convinced... they'd have a wider appeal... if they were smaller...
Picasso	Smaller feet... it's noted. Thank you Herr Frisch.

Picasso is moving the paintings with difficulty – some of them are heavy and awkward

Having put back 'The Lovers', he turns his attention to the next painting

He pulls out painting of 'The Weeping Woman' and holds it upright on the floor

Picasso   Well, well! This is where you've been hiding.

Hebbel   The original two-eyed monster eh. Bits where she shouldn't have. (*He laughs*)

Picasso   (*Building up to an angry passion*) Not if you look. I looked - from different angles. I painted from more than one of them! I threw my angles on the canvas! I said balls to the single-view, I said sod off perspective! Titian and Raphael and Rembrandt worked that seam! Let's have multi-dimensional, multi-angled art that says something. Let's follow our urge. LET'S GO WHERE IT LEADS. THIS IS WHERE IT LED. BEYOND THE TRIED AND TESTED. INTO THE UNKNOWN.

Pause

Hebbel	You went with your feelings then.
Picasso	With every fibre in my body, monsieur! And above all with my soul!

Hebbel measures it

Picasso	She's beautiful. We're having difficulty living together.
Hebbel	200 by 45.
Frisch	(*As he writes*) Two...hundred...by...
Hebbel	You like women.
Picasso	Too much.
Hebbel	D'you want to see some? Bella ragazza.

Hebbel feels in his inside jacket pocket. He takes a packet out, opens it. It's full of photographs

	Paint women like this you can charge what you like! (*Picasso makes sounds of approval*) Wouldn't you give a week's pay for a night with her?
Picasso	She'd have to come cheap with what I get in a week.

Hebbel	Get the violins out, Monsieur's so poor he can't afford a night with a beautiful woman - even though he's the most famous artist in the world. Have you seen these Willi? Have a butcher's.
Frisch	Seen one you've seen them all.
Hebbel	Not this one! Athletic or what?
Frisch	(*Frisch looks*) Very nice.
Hebbel	You didn't look! Look at that body. Those muscles.
Frisch	I'm looking. Okay! (*Stares hard at photo*)
Hebbel	That's right, feast your eyes.
Frisch	I don't know why you've still got them.
Hebbel	(*Next photo in pile*) What d'you think of this sexy lady in a hat?
Frisch	You're meant to hand them in... all goods confiscated in the line of duty...
Hebbel	Don't tell me about goods. I know about goods. I've been doing this for as long as you. These are snaps. They're not goods.

Picasso decides to put the painting back

Frisch　　　　　You took those from a Frenchman.

Hebbel　　　　(*Mimics*) 'You took those from a Frenchman.' How d'you know what he was?

Frisch　　　　　I saw his identity card.

Hebbel　　　　They can be forged.

Frisch　　　　　He had a French name. He looked French.

Hebbel　　　　He looked French. What a load of nonsense. What can you tell by looks? Take Herr Picasso here. He might be Spanish... or he might not be.

Picasso　　　　I very much am.

Hebbel walks up to Picasso, studies his face

Hebbel　　　　You may very well be... (*Looks at Picasso's nose*) but... what sort of nose is this? Is this a Spanish nose? Or a Jewish nose. Or is it a gypsy nose - you've got thousands in Spain.

Picasso　　　　I am from the Ruiz of Malaga. Of pure Spanish stock. My name is Pablo Diego

> Jose Francisco de Paula Juan Nepomuceno Maria de los Remedios Crispiniano de la Santisma Trinidad Ruiz y Picasso. I defy you to get more Spanish than that.

Hebbel …How would we know? Not by looking, that's for sure. One has to study the family tree – that's the only way. People in Paris are in for a shock soon I tell you. You're going to have to prove your blood-line, generations back… so there's no miscegenation.

Picasso slots painting back

Picasso I've got nothing to fear.

Hebbel Didn't think for a moment you had. The Spanish and the Germans - like that. (*Crosses fingers*)

Picasso starts to extricate next painting

Picasso …You hear funny stories about people and their race…

Hebbel Mm?

Picasso You know what I heard the other day? An artist had some works taken. In Paris. Yes.

	Had his paintings logged... and then they took them.
Hebbel	Who did?
Picasso	The Germans.
Hebbel	Must've been a criminal.
Picasso	He wasn't.
Hebbel	A spy then...
Frisch	...Communist.
Picasso	I heard because of his race.
Hebbel	You know what I say? There are too many rumours buzzing around, 'specially in times like these. Best ignore them.
Picasso	Seems a funny thing to do...
Hebbel	Unless he painted women as sexy as these! (*He slaps photos and laughs loudly*) Then you could understand them taking them. For a private look? All by themselves?
Picasso	Everyone wants to get their hands on a lovely woman, one way or another.

Hebbel	Anyway no one's taking anything from you monsieur Picasso. You don't have to worry about that.

Picasso extricates a painting. He talks as he does

Picasso	I had a visit from some Germans last week. Came to my studio, looking for a Lipschitz. I'd never heard of him. It wasn't a name I knew. One of them asked me if I was a Jew. Why would they ask me that?
Hebbel	You get funny sorts in all nations. Even ours. Best to ignore them.
Frisch	You need to worry more about what they think of your art than your race.
Hebbel	(*He winks broadly*) An artist they didn't like… say a degenerate Bolshevik… or a Bolshevik-degenerate… one influenced by the Talmud say… he'd have to keep an eye on things. (*Suddenly relaxes and laughs*) Or someone might take his stuff. Without asking.
Frisch	And once they were taken, who knows when you'd see them again.

Picasso ignores these remarks. He has the next painting out. He leans it up for Hebbel and Frisch to see

Hebbel   Well, well. What have we here?

Frisch   A circus.

Hebbel   So it is. With an acrobat. And horses. And a ring-master

Frisch   Reminds me of when I was a kid. We used to go to the circus.

A calculating glint comes into Picasso's eyes

Picasso   If you could look at this painting every day would it bring back those memories?

Frisch   Yes.

Hebbel   Ask Monsieur Picasso nicely he might sell you it, Willi.

Frisch   I think not Franz.

Picasso   You won't know if you don't ask.

Frisch   On a soldier's wages?

Hebbel	A soldier's wages are better than nothing to a painter who can't sell a thing.
Picasso	D'you like the painting Monsieur Frisch?
Frisch	Yes I do.
Picasso	Two thousand it's yours.
Frisch	Two thousand did you say?
Hebbel	What a price.
Picasso	Can't you afford it? Is it too dear?
Frisch	Well I... you'll sell me this painting for two thousand francs?
Picasso	That's what I said.
Hebbel	There - what did I tell you?
Frisch	But it's so cheap.
Hebbel	Haven't you got two grand, Willi?
Frisch	Of course I've got two grand.
Hebbel	Then what are you waiting for?

Frisch	You know damn well what.
Hebbel	I don't. I can't see why you don't jump at the chance to own a lovely painting by Herr Picasso.
Frisch	You do Willi but I'll tell you anyway. Say Kimmert gets to know about it?
Hebbel	So what if he does? What's the problem?
Frisch	Well that I...
Picasso	...Bought a painting? It's not wrong is it? Are you telling me a soldier can't buy things, with his money, that he's put his life at risk for?
Frisch	...The price is so low he'll...
Hebbel	He'll what?
Frisch	...Be suspicious.
Hebbel	I can't see why.
Frisch	...He'll think it's strange.
Hebbel	Monsieur Picasso has asked for a price, above board and legal! He should know

	what he's doing! Lots of his paintings aren't worth what he's asked you for that one, are they Monsieur Picasso?
Picasso	The frames are worth more than the paintings with some of them.
Hebbel	There. See, he's pleased to sell to anyone. Stop fretting. Give him the money.
Frisch	Why don't you buy it, if you're so keen?
Hebbel	It's not been offered to me.
Picasso	You've said nice things about my work, Herr Frisch. Please take it.
Frisch	I'd love to... but... I can't.
Picasso	I'll be insulted.
Frisch	No... please. I am not insulting you. That's the last thing in the world I would do.
Picasso	To a Spaniard refusing an offer is an insult.
Hebbel	Insulting Herr Picasso, Frisch? And you such an admirer of his.

Picasso	(*Tempting him*) Take it. I'm giving you it. Just hold out your hand and it's yours.

Picasso forces Frisch to take and hold the painting

Frisch	(*Looking at it*) It's nice... a nice work.
Picasso	...A small work.
Frisch	I can't. I really... back me Franz.
Hebbel	Not if you're upsetting monsieur Picasso.
Frisch	Here monsieur. I'm putting it down. Carefully...

Frisch very carefully puts painting on floor, leaning it against a pile of other paintings

Picasso	It doesn't take a second to say yes.
Frisch	I can't buy your painting. I simply can't. For god's sake can we get on!
Picasso	How about I up it to two thousand two hundred then. Is that any better?

Frisch pushes on into the depths of the vault

Hebbel	Where are you going?

Frisch	To see what paintings are out the back.
Hebbel	We can't log, then. You've got the book.
Frisch	Then wait. I want an idea of how many we've got to get through.
Hebbel	Don't start an avalanche.

Frisch picks his way carefully along the wall, treading over and between paintings till he disappears from view

Hebbel	There a kazi down here?
Picasso	Upstairs.
Hebbel	Or find a corner eh.
Picasso	You won't be the first.
Hebbel	Might as well have a break. Till he gets back. I'll hold it in.

Hebbel takes a spirit flask out of his jacket pocket. He takes a swig, smacks his lips

From now on Hebbel and Picasso talk in whispers

Picasso	(*Quiet*) Is your colleague okay? He looked a bit...

Hebbel	(*Also quiet*) He's only okay when he's not okay - if you get my drift.
Picasso	(*Quiet*) Nothing I said then?
Hebbel	(*Quiet*) He upsets himself! He wants that painting but he won't let himself.
Picasso	Does it break some army-rule?
Hebbel	We're supposed to keep everything strictly honest. No deals. No barter. No gifts.
Picasso	It was spur-of-the-moment. I wouldn't want to get him into trouble.
Hebbel	Think no more about it. That's Frisch. He goes to extremes - 'specially when he's being honest.
Picasso	...S'pose you can't blame him.
Hebbel	Can't I? Try working with him!
Picasso	...He seems efficient.
Hebbel	Like Jesus efficient. He won't take an elastic band without logging it in triplicate.
Picasso	As you say - honest.

Hebbel	He makes the rest of us feel like shit. Not honest to goodness smelly shit. Cheap shit.
Picasso	...Not so good...
Hebbel	Where's the harm in taking a few photos, or the odd pair of nylons? But not saint Willi. He won't soil his hands with a tin tack.
Picasso	A true disciple in his honesty.
Hebbel	I wouldn't call it that.
Picasso	You wouldn't?
Hebbel	If it was honesty I'd respect him. No, he wants the stuff but he's scared of getting caught. Then he won't get promoted and his halo'll drop off.
Picasso	Fear of getting caught... desire to be honest. Difficult to tell apart.
Hebbel	No one likes working with him. You have to be dead careful what you do because you can't get back at him, you've nothing on him. He never does anything wrong ...'cept not like women.
Picasso	That's wrong is it?

Hebbel	Not wrong. Not normal.
Picasso	I'm a free spirit where people's preferences are concerned.
Hebbel	Me too. He could be the biggest homo in the German army for all I care - if he'd just stop being so high and mighty.
Picasso	The same school eh?
Hebbel	How d'you think we speak such good French?
Picasso	I wondered about that.
Hebbel	We come from Strasbourg. Half its life it's been French, half, German. Half of us have got French names, half they're German. You got German speakers and French speakers and some of us who can speak both. We've all got a bit of each other in us. We're all a bit confused about who we are. I'm glad we've stopped killing each other.
Picasso	Were you mates back then?
Hebbel	I was in the year above. 'S where we... he was a bit more like the rest of us then. We spent a lot of time together... fencing...

	circuits... bit of horse-riding... great times... bloody great...
Picasso	You don't now?
Hebbel	You got to move with the times Herr Picasso. You join the army, you have to muck in. You can't be talking about art and novels all the time. In front of the blokes. It irritates them. They think you're lording it. And you certainly can't have a mate pose for you. While you draw them. Even if there's nothing in it.
Picasso	Did Herr Frisch...?
Hebbel	People talk. You get labelled. Then you'd better watch yourself. So... you either go with the flow or you end up...
Picasso	On the outside?
Hebbel	...Looking in. I went with the flow. I made the odd remark, with the lads. Before I know it Willi and me are hardly what you could call mates anymore. Then one day he tells me he's destroyed his work. Every last drawing. He won't tell me how, just he has. Bloody waste really. (*Silence*) Great price you gave him for the painting.

Picasso	(*Glint again*) When someone likes what I do it puts me in a generous mood.
Hebbel	(*Shouts*) Frischy!
Frisch	(*Shouts*) There's another big roomful!
Hebbel	(*Shouts*) We need to get on!
Frisch	(*Shouts*) And don't call me Frischy.
Hebbel	(*Shouts*) How many you counted?
Frisch	(*Shouts*) If you let me get on I might be able to tell you.

Hebbel drinks from his flask again

Hebbel	This lot's going to take forever. Speed we're moving.
Picasso	I'd er... love to knock this off quickly.
Hebbel	Me too. Can't stand hanging around on a job.
Picasso	I've got so many other things to do.

Hebbel sizes Picasso up, takes a decision

Hebbel	(*Thinks*) ...If you're sharp you can work a trick... to make time. If you're not a follower of Saint Paul of Frisch that is.
Picasso	Go on.
Hebbel	They give you a job. Off you trot. You work your hours. End of day one, you report back. 'There's a lot more work than we thought, sir. We need two more days, sir.' But you work it so you only need one.
Picasso	So you make a day.
Hebbel	Free time, for yourself.
Picasso	I could do with some of that.

Hebbel again drinks from flask. Wipes lips

Picasso	Realistically, there's three days work here. At least.
Hebbel	Jesus that much?
Picasso	This is art. You can't be flinging this around like crates of beer.
Hebbel	Long as I get away by six today.

Picasso	I want to get away too.
Hebbel	I'm meeting a woman.
Picasso	I'm meeting a woman as well. A beautiful young woman.
Hebbel	Sexy is she?
Picasso	She's deep and complicated. When she's in the mood she takes me to paradise and keeps me there a very long time.
Hebbel	You randy bastard.
Picasso	And yours? What's she like?
Hebbel	What she doesn't know about love-making isn't worth knowing. I want to marry her after the war.
Picasso	(*Remembering*) I thought you said you had a...?
Hebbel	Did I? Well I do. That's the problem.
Picasso	Divorce is it? Or bigamy?
Hebbel	I thank and curse this war. If it hadn't been for it, I wouldn't've met Thérèse and I'd

	still be happily married to my wife. Then again I wouldn't've missed meeting Thérèse for anything.
Picasso	We men - we get thrown into these situations.
Hebbel	Now I'm an adulterer, a cheat and a liar and all because of a sodding war.
Picasso	Caught between two women you like.
Hebbel	Two women I love.
Picasso	I know the feeling.
Hebbel	You?
Picasso	In the same fix. Two women together. One dark and dangerous, the other blonde and sensual. Both wonderful in different ways.
Hebbel	Got any tips?
Picasso	Learn to juggle.
Hebbel	Between countries.

Picasso	(*After short silence*) ...You know I reckon you could work that trick. The one you said...
Hebbel	Talk to me tomorrow.
Picasso	In fact... we could finish today.
Hebbel	All this? You got a magic wand?
Picasso	Something much more simple. I give you one price for everything that's left.
Hebbel	One price the lot?
Picasso	A job-lot price. By the end of today you'll have the best ones done - the rest are rubbish.
Hebbel	I can quote you on that?
Picasso	Apprentice works. No one's going to bother about them - they're worth zilch. We can zip through them at thirty an hour...
Hebbel	...'S tempting.
Picasso	I'm happy to do it.
Hebbel	...Problem... Oberstleutnant Kimmert.

Picasso	If Kimmert says anything, you tell him to talk to me. I'm the expert.
Hebbel	If only I could.
Picasso	I'll answer any questions.
Hebbel	Anyway it's not just Kimmert - we could maybe get round him. It's Frisch. He'll want to log every item, including empty frames and dead rats.
Picasso	That's a bit awkward. Let me think... see what I can... let's see... let's see... yes. A germ of an idea!
Hebbel	Spit it out.
Picasso	It's good.
Hebbel	Don't hold back.
Picasso	I think it'll work...
Hebbel	Don't keep me in suspense a second longer.
Picasso	...No.
Hebbel	No what?

Picasso	You wouldn't do it.
Hebbel	Wouldn't do what?
Picasso	You wouldn't have the face.
Hebbel	I've got face, oh believe me I've got face enough for a hundred Germans. Tell me what you're thinking.
Picasso	This is how it works. We tell Frisch that Kimmert doesn't WANT you to log all my works. We say Kimmert WANTS a job-lot price.
Hebbel	(*Puzzled*) Based on what do we tell him that?
Picasso	(*Thinking on feet*) ...Based on... the fact I'm well-known in America and the last thing Kimmert and the high-ups want is the Americans upset. For diplomatic reasons. To do with the war. And they will be upset if you're harassing me.
Hebbel	We wouldn't dream of harassing you, Herr Picasso.

Picasso	I'm not saying you are. I'm talking tactics. How we work on Herr Frisch... so he gets a shift on... to everyone's benefit. (*Wink*)
Hebbel	(*Thinking*) ...I know him. He'll just say why didn't Kimmert make it clear to us before we came.
Picasso	He will? Yes... um... let me think... mmm... let's see... (*Idea arrives*) How about we say Kimmert did make it clear?
Hebbel	He didn't make it clear to me.
Picasso	Yes he did! In a SUBTLE way. By dropping hints. Frisch didn't pick up on them but you did. ...Just to prove it you remember them as I drop them into the conversation.
Hebbel	Getting better.
Picasso	In fact... yes oh yes - how about this for a piece of cheek? I tell Frisch I KNOW Kimmert. Personally. As a friend. But it's hush-hush on account of he can't be seen to mix with me because officially I'm a degenerate so he has to work through hints. You act like you believe every word I say. Frisch'll be wondering now... thinking...

	did I miss something... maybe getting scared. He won't want a fight if he thinks it'll upset Kimmert.
Hebbel	Hmm... it might work.
Picasso	We've got nothing to lose - we men of the world (*Wink*) - if we want our day off.
Hebbel	Will Frisch take the bait? I lay money he'll be back in the office tonight. 'Oberstleutnant Kimmert, I'm a good boy. We've done it as a job-lot price like you wanted and now I'm reporting for more work, sir.'
Picasso	We need a clincher. To stop that.
Hebbel	Hold on... yes! Maybe I've got it. (*He listens to make sure Frisch is nowhere near. Quiet voice*) Will I enjoy this! I tell Herr Frisch he goes along with our plans or Kimmert hears about him taking bribes.
Picasso	I thought you said he was bribeless.
Hebbel	The painting... the circus one.
Picasso	(*Innocently*) What of it?

Hebbel	He tried to make you give it to him...
Picasso	He didn't. He wouldn't even take it when I offered it to him.
Hebbel	That's not how I remember it.
Picasso	You saw him. He told me he couldn't take it because... (*Stops*) Oh. Oh oh. Ah. (*Realisation*) Right. I see where you're heading.
Hebbel	He put pressure on you to give it to him for nothing?
Picasso	Yes...
Hebbel	...But I stepped in.
Picasso	Maybe you did.
Hebbel	...And told him it was against the rules... and shameful for a German soldier to behave like that.
Picasso	I'm beginning to remember now... yes... you did...

Picasso stares at Hebbel. Hebbel looks at Picasso

Hebbel	I don't want this job to drag. I've got things to do. So have you. What d'you say to my suggestion?
Picasso	Well... why not? (*Thought*) Is that why you were so keen on Herr Frisch buying that painting from me? So you could say he...? (*Hebbel taps side of nose with finger*) That's what I call thinking ahead...
Hebbel	What about you? Did you offer him that painting out of the goodness of your heart?
Picasso	Put it this way - I don't usually give my paintings away without good reason.
Hebbel	(*Smiles then serious*) Ah. I've just thought - if you're supposed to know Kimmert, I bet Frisch'll ask you what he looks like.
Picasso	Well remembered. How could I not think of that? What does he look like?
Hebbel	Impeccable. Never a stain or crease in his gear... Medium build. Thin. Long nose. Birth-mark half way down his cheek - like someone's slapped a great blob of raspberry jam on. Tries to hide it.

Hebbel mimics keeping right side of his face away from Picasso

Picasso	Now I know all that, I'm confident.
Hebbel	Yes... this could work. Tell you what - why don't I disappear when he comes back? Find a wall, have that piss. Leave you with him. You can chat. Make friends...
Picasso	Better to know your man if you want to turn him?
Hebbel	If you get some juicy gossip you tell me. I'll save it up for the next ruck.
Picasso	I will.
Hebbel	You're on.

Hebbel swigs back brandy from flask

        Brandy? Spark us up a bit?

Picasso takes offered flask. Takes a good mouthful

They hear Frisch making his way back

Hebbel	Willi, you decided to come back. You been in a war?
Frisch	It's dangerous out there.

Frisch is dirty. He has dust and distemper over his uniform

He brushes himself down painstakingly with his hands

Hebbel	For a brave soldier like yourself?
Frisch	You think this is bad, wait till you get back there. Paintings everywhere.
Hebbel	How many rows are we talking?
Frisch	Twenty. Thirty. If you can call them rows. They're all over the place.
Hebbel	How many paintings per row?
Frisch	God knows.
Hebbel	He does but do you?
Frisch	Twenty... at a guess.
Hebbel	...Forty per row - that's eight hundred of the buggers. We'd better bring our sleeping-bags.

Hebbel takes a bar of chocolate out of a pocket. Unwraps it, takes a bite

Hebbel	Chocolate, monsieur?

Picasso stops pulling out painting, takes a piece of chocolate, eats it

Hebbel   Willi?

Frisch   Thanks.

All three contentedly eat chocolate

Picasso   Mmmm. Nice.

Hebbel   (*To Frisch*) D'you bring any food?

Frisch   No.

Hebbel   We'll be hungry, time we leave. Not before ten o'clock by my reckoning.

Frisch   Ten?

Hebbel   Earliest.

Frisch   Better get on then.

Picasso   I'm ready.

Picasso pulls out next painting

Picasso   Oh oh. What have we here?

Hebbel	One sad-looking bastard.
Picasso	I've caught his likeness.
Hebbel	Just lost a fortune had he? Mother died?
Picasso	He'd spent the day with me.
Frisch	Ha ha. Title?
Picasso	'Loyal Clerk'.
Hebbel	Price?
Picasso	Eight thousand francs. Jaime's the only one who'd buy it and he's as poor as the rest of us.

Hebbel measures it

Hebbel   70 by 68!

Frisch writes dimensions in book, murmuring them as he does

Picasso pushes painting back. He struggles

Hebbel   I need to water a wall. Don't do anything till I get back.

Hebbel goes back out by exit to vault corridor. We hear his footsteps echo as he walks away

Picasso lights up a cigarette

Frisch takes a pack of cigarettes out of his pocket

Picasso   No ash on my paintings.

Frisch   No... no. I'll be careful. Flick it well away.

Frisch lights up. They smoke

Frisch brushes himself down every now and then, tugs creases out of uniform obsessively

Picasso   Dirty job.

Frisch   Very.

Picasso   The pulling and pushing. The dust and droppings. The bloody fingers.

Frisch   Least I get to see lots of paintings.

Picasso   Can I ask you something - artist to artist?

Frisch   I'm not an artist.

Picasso   Anyone who paints is an artist.

Frisch	I didn't paint - I drew.
Picasso	Painting... drawing... it's all art.
Frisch	If that's your definition then I suppose I'm an artist.
Picasso	A good one by the sounds of it. Win any competitions?
Frisch	I won the art-prize every year in school. By a margin.
Picasso	I feel I'm talking to a kindred spirit.
Frisch	I hope so.
Picasso	What's the reason? For this?
Frisch	(*Quiet voice*) This...?
Picasso	(*Quiet voice*) Yes this. The real reason?
Frisch	(*Quiet voice*) It's not just you. Every artist in Paris is having it done.
Picasso	(*Quiet*) But what's it for? All these old works. Even I'd forgotten I had some of 'em.

Frisch — ...We're like that. A thorough nation. Everything in order. In every country we liberate. That's how we are. We want to be able to put our hand on anything, wherever and whenever we want. It's a good way to run a country.

He takes a deep draw on his cigarette

Frisch — Artists should be grateful. It's work we're doing for them, this listing and logging. Gratis.

Picasso — Artists I know are worried.

Frisch — There's no need.

Picasso — Do I need to worry?

Frisch — No.

Picasso — You're sure?

Frisch — As far as I know...

Picasso — As far as you know? Well how far is as far as you know, Herr Frisch?

Frisch — I know a bit.

Picasso	D'you know what they're thinking? The ones at the top? Is that something you would know? They've whispered in your ear?
Frisch	In kinds of ways... if you know what I mean.
Picasso	No I don't know what you mean.
Frisch	I can't say outright.
Picasso	Herr Frisch eh... the artists' friend. I bet their eyes light up when you walk through the door.
Frisch	They would if they knew me.
Picasso	Why did they take that artist's paintings? Can you tell me?
Frisch	Not unless you give me more details.
Picasso	How did he upset them? Hair the wrong colour? Feet too big? But you wouldn't know would you?
Frisch	Not without names and dates.

Picasso	Thanks for trying so hard to help me. I appreciate that. What I expect from a fellow artist.
Frisch	Look… if I tell you something…?
Picasso	But you've already told me everything.
Frisch	Well… maybe not everything.
Picasso	Then I'm all ears.
Frisch	Give me your word it stays between us.
Picasso	My word of honour. As a free-born Spaniard and artist of the world.

Frisch looks around, listens, making sure Hebbel is nowhere near. Quiet voice

Frisch	…They take some artists' works… a few.
Picasso	Take them where?
Frisch	I don't know.
Picasso	You don't know?
Frisch	No.

Picasso	Why do they?
Frisch	You probably know as much as me.
Picasso	All I know are rumours.
Frisch	Then you probably know more than me.
Picasso	For exhibitions? Isn't that what you said?
Frisch	Hebbel said.
Picasso	You don't sound so sure.
Frisch	It's what I'd hope.
Picasso	It's no more than that? A hope?
Frisch	Time will tell.
Picasso	So you do this job but you've precious little idea why you're doing it?
Frisch	I was encouraged to volunteer. When you're asked, god help you if you say no.
Picasso	You must've wondered about it. What purpose it serves? You knock on artists' doors, you drag them off to their studios

	and storage-places, at all hours, and you don't have the faintest idea why?
Frisch	Maybe security. In case their works go missing.
Picasso	Or maybe because they're Jewish? Could that be it? My friend was Jewish. A French Jewish artist. Did that have anything to do with it?
Frisch	If it did, it's a funny basis on which to take away someone's works.
Picasso	What about artists like me - the degenerates. What plans do they have for my works?
Frisch	I've told you Herr Picasso, you're too famous for them to upset.
Picasso	Can you give me proof?
Frisch	…Officer Kimmert said in our briefing, we had to be careful not to do anything that put you in a bad mood.
Picasso	You heard him say that?

Frisch	Not two hours ago. As clear as I'm hearing you.
Picasso	He probably says that about every artist you visit.
Frisch	In general we try to keep things calm. In that sense you're right. But for you it was stronger. He repeated it a number of times.
Picasso	D'you enjoy your work?
Frisch	It beats a lot of what's on offer. Anyway once they found out I knew a bit about art...
Picasso	I can see why they chose you. You understand artists.
Frisch	I try to.
Picasso	You know about art.
Frisch	A bit more than the average.
Picasso	A bit more than you let on. Wouldn't surprise me if you knew a lot about my art.
Frisch	If I did I've forgotten it.

Picasso	My pink period? D'you like that? You love circus people? Acrobats. Clowns…
Frisch	They're a favourite subject. If I could only draw them like…
Picasso	…Me?

Frisch realises Picasso's 'trapped' him. Embarrassed, he stays silent

Picasso	And Herr Hebbel? He a reluctant recruit too?
Frisch	You'll have to ask him.
Picasso	He doesn't know the first thing about art. So why does he talk to you like you're an ignoramus?
Frisch	He talks to me with respect about art.
Picasso	Believe that if you want.
Frisch	…How does he talk to me then?
Picasso	Like he's the boss, and you're his ignorant little apprentice.

Frisch	Who cares? I can shut him up whenever I feel like it.
Picasso	Is that so?
Frisch	Just like that! (*Clicks fingers again*)
Picasso	Well... must be good... knowing you can.
Frisch	It's very good. Very good indeed.
Picasso	Nice feeling... It's there if you want it.
Frisch	I call it my secret weapon.
Picasso	To be brought out exactly when you want.
Frisch	That's it.
Picasso	I'd love to know what it is - your secret weapon. But that's being nosey...
Frisch	He knows if he pushes me too far I'll tell Oberstleutnant Kimmert about his constant thieving.
Picasso	But you're biding your time? Till the right moment?

Frisch	I don't want to drag myself down to his level unless l have to and I don't have to right now.
Picasso	Monsieur Frisch I like you. You're a decent young man. You've got the soul of an artist. Please take this painting. (*Holds out circus painting to Frisch*) Please. If not now I'll send it to you in Germany. Write your address.

Picasso gets paper and pencil out of his overcoat pocket

Frisch	That's very generous... but I can't.
Picasso	I'll take risks for someone I like.
Frisch	You can't. I can't. That would be...!
Picasso	Take it now. I'll wrap it in paper. If Hebbel says anything, unleash your secret weapon - the one you just told me about. I'll weigh in on your side.

Picasso starts to wrap newspaper round picture

Frisch	It's not as easy as that.

Picasso	We can't let him stop you taking presents from an artist you like and who likes you. I won't let him.
Frisch	Ssssh. Here he is.

We hear footsteps from corridor area. They get louder. Hebbel enters

Hebbel	No one can say I'm full of piss now!
Picasso	Your ears must be burning!
Hebbel	Someone did?
Frisch	Full of something a lot more solid than piss!
Hebbel	I had a good dump too so I'm not full of that either! Right, fellow plotters, no time to lose. Monsieur, if you'll do the honours.

Picasso turns his attention to getting out a painting

He does lots of grunting and groaning

Hebbel	What the hell's that bull doing with that girl?
Picasso	Impregnating a nymph with the seed of the gods.

Hebbel	Bloody perverted. That's... I mean that's impossible isn't it?
Frisch	Title?
Hebbel	I asked Herr Picasso a question.
Frisch	Can we have the title please?
Picasso	Randy Minotaur.
Hebbel	It wouldn't fit surely...
Frisch	Price?
Picasso	Only eight thousand. People are easily shocked.

Frisch writes. Hebbel measures

Hebbel	80 by 68.

Picasso slots it back

Suddenly he starts back with a cry, wringing his hand

Picasso	Owh! God! Aah!
Hebbel	What is it? What's the matter?

Picasso	Wrist. Aah! Jesus. My painting arm.
Frisch	What's the matter with it?
Picasso	Owh. Shit! Mmm.
Hebbel	Amputation is it? I know a good butcher. No one can hold a cleaver up to him.
Frisch	Can we help? Shall I get a doctor?
Picasso	I didn't do it on purpose if that's what you think.
Frisch	I never thought that...
Picasso	It goes. All of a sudden. One minute it's strong then click, no strength in the fingers. Believe me.
Frisch	No, when I asked about a doctor I was worried...
Hebbel	...About the job, eh Willi? How we'll get it finished before Christmas? Couldn't care less Monsieur's hurt himself, just worried about slowing the pace. I know how your mind works.

Frisch	What would be best for Monsieur? How about if I moved the paintings? If I promise to be careful. Would that help?
Picasso	I can't have anyone touch my paintings. It's too risky. I'll just have to…

Picasso tries to move a painting. Howls, grunts, squeals

Picasso	Ooh. Ah…
Frisch	Slow down. Rest your hand. Don't force it.

Picasso sits with much ado

Frisch	I get the same with my wrist. I bent it hard back when I was a kid and now if I jerk it it can go weak as water.
Hebbel	Like me with my ear. Teacher pulled it hard cos I coughed in his class - now it flaps about like a rag.
Frisch	Very funny Franz.

All three men stop what they're doing. Picasso sits on frame of painting. Frisch and Hebbel stand

Picasso	So much of the stuff. So many to do…

Silence

Hebbel I've got a suggestion. To help monsieur because he's in no fit state to be lugging pictures round. Willi, you listening?

Frisch Actually I was thinking.

Hebbel Stop before you hurt your brain. (*Clears throat*) This is what I think. It's just come to me. In a blinding flash. Why doesn't Monsieur Picasso give us one price for the ones we haven't done? That way he needn't touch another painting and we needn't bother him to touch one either. Would that be possible monsieur?

Picasso Well... I don't see why not...

Hebbel Excellent! I reckon that's a bloody good solution.

Frisch Just one thing Franz. What about Kimmert?

Hebbel What about him?

Frisch He won't accept that. He'll go mad if he finds out.

Hebbel	Don't care about Herr Picasso then, Willi. What if he's in agony? Who cares if his wrist's broken - let's break it some more. Let's make him damage it so much he never ever paints again!

We see Picasso stand with great difficulty – he's laying it on thick

Frisch	I didn't mean...
Picasso	(*Holding one hand in other*) Owh. Ugh. Jesus! Such pain.
Frisch	(*To Picasso*) ...you to move them Monsieur. It's just if you knew Oberstleutnant Kimmert...
Picasso	I do.
Frisch	...You'd know why we're worried. If you don't do exactly what he says, when he... (*Pause. He realises*) What did you say? About Officer Kimmert?
Picasso	I know him.
Frisch	You know Kimmert?
Picasso	For the third time, yes.

Frisch	Art Division Reichsdirektorate Kimmert?
Picasso	YES.
Hebbel	Good god! Well I... That is a... Have you known him for long?
Picasso	I can't say.
Hebbel	Of course you can't! Of course he can't. What a dumb question.
Picasso	It wouldn't be right.
Hebbel	Stands to reason. A child could see that. Don't push it Willi.
Frisch	That's amazing. You know our commanding officer?
Picasso	Why'd'you say it like that? D'you think I'm lying?
Frisch	No! Absolutely not. It's just...
Picasso	I know him pretty well. Me and him are pretty good mates... what with that mark on his face, and that lavender cologne he splashes on. He must use gallons of the stuff.

Hebbel	Lavender cologne? But I... you know about that?
Picasso	How could you not know? It fair takes your breath away.
Hebbel	But how do you...? (*Stops*) Well yes... yes it does take your breath away.
Picasso	(*Interrupting*) And have you noticed how bothered he is about that birth-mark? Well of course you have - you work with him. Does he give orders sideways on? Like this. (*Picasso mimics man hiding one side of his face*)
Frisch	He does yes.
Hebbel	(*Still puzzled*) Fancy you know Kimmert wears lavender cologne.
Picasso	The way the poor man holds his face. He moves round to the left, so you move to the right. Round and round in circles.
Frisch	God that's...
Hebbel	Kimmert! No doubt about it. You're full of surprises Herr Picasso.

Frisch	I'm gobsmacked.
Picasso	I can't go into details but I know this for a fact - he doesn't want you logging all my works. In fact it's the last thing he wants.
Frisch	But he told us... to log everything.
Picasso	Sounds to me like you took him at face-value. Knowing Herr Kimmert, he'd've said one thing but meant another. With hints. He's a master of the hint. Didn't you pick up on them?
Frisch	Well I... did you Franz?
Hebbel	Now Monsieur mentions it, maybe I did. Yes... Being quick with the job, not giving cause for complaint...
Picasso	Exactly! Why'd'you think I was expecting you when you rang me?
Frisch	I didn't think you were. You seemed pretty surprised when you picked up the phone.
Picasso	I'd been warned... by a certain person. Do I make myself clear?
Frisch	Why didn't you tell us this before?

Picasso	THINK about it! Consider Herr Kimmert's position. He can't have the whole world knowing what company he keeps - company that may not be APPROVED. I was hoping I wouldn't have to spell this out.
Hebbel	Kimmert won't thank us for making you.
Frisch	I had no idea about this.
Picasso	I can understand. Sometimes hints are difficult to pick up. 'Specially these days. They have to be so subtle you wonder if there was a hint at all.
Hebbel	That's settled then - one price for the lot. Give us the price Herr Picasso!
Picasso	...Say one hundred and sixty thousand francs. Plus the ones you've logged already. Gives a nice mix.
Frisch	I was sure we were meant to price each painting separately.
Hebbel	Herr Picasso has just explained.
Frisch	Say we get this wrong?

Hebbel	Herr Picasso has just told you he's a friend of Kimmert's. D'you doubt his word?
Frisch	Not for a second.
Hebbel	So what's your problem?
Frisch	I wish I felt more confident...
Hebbel	Alright, how about this? We work hard for the rest of the day. Log as many as we can. Then a job-lot price for what's left. That way it's a half-way house. Half done separate, half as a lot.
Frisch	You know what happened to Karsters? He got caught trying this on. You know where he is now.
Hebbel	Behind bars where he should be. Karsters is thick. He couldn't organise a blind date for a nun. Don't compare me with Karsters. So we log a few more and finish?
Picasso	If that's what you want.
Hebbel	Into action! A last burst and we're done.

Picasso walks along a row. He pulls out a painting, holding open a gap with his leg

Frisch   I'm not sure about...

Picasso   Mother and Child. 1930.

Picasso pulls out another painting

           Sexy Lady. Pen and ink.

Frisch   ...this. I don't see why we can't...

Hebbel   70 by 160. Willi, wake up! Get this down now.

Picasso shoves this one back and immediately pulls out the next

Picasso   Me in 1906. What an enigmatic bastard.

Picasso shoves it back and pulls out the next

           Man on a Wall, oil, 1905.

           The same

Hebbel   (*Two paintings behind*) Are you getting these? 20 by 35 for Sexy Lady. 100 by 150 for Monsieur by himself. The bloke on the wall, 70 by 85.

Frisch   Can you slow down?

Picasso	I'm in a rhythm.
Frisch	Is your wrist better?
Picasso	It must've been a trapped tendon. One minute it's agony, the next like it didn't happen.
Hebbel	All oil on canvas are they?
Picasso	All but the Sexy Lady. She's pen and ink.
Hebbel	Date painted?
Picasso	Nineteen thirty. Twenty eight. Thirty five. Twenty one.
Frisch	Look I just can't… Can you help me log Franz? We'll keep a steady pace then.
Picasso	Excellent idea! With the two of you we'll skate along.
Hebbel	It'll cost you.
Frisch	Why should I have to…
Hebbel	Two packs of ciggies.
Frisch	I've only got one.

Hebbel   Two's my final offer.

Picasso sets off at a hell of a pace, pulling out paintings and pushing them back almost immediately. Incredible din of bashing and crashing

Picasso   Man with Stallion... 1908. Fruit and Harmonica on Grey Table. When did I paint that? No idea. Oh look at that... just look will you... (*Painting slams back*)

Frisch   I didn't see.

Picasso   I thought we were to do this at speed? Am I going too fast?

Hebbel   Not for me. You go as fast as you like.

Picasso pulls out next painting

Picasso   Memories... what memories. Saltimbanques... mmm...

Frisch   Franz please. I know you've got your book.

Hebbel   You know my terms.

Frisch bangs into a painting with his leg

Frisch   Ouch! My sodding leg. Shit!

Picasso	Watch my painting!
Hebbel	Careful what you kick!
Frisch	Look, if I give you one pack now and one next week when I get my pay.
Hebbel	They're not poor quality?
Frisch	They're Sobranie.
Hebbel	You're on. Rendez-vous with Thérèse tonight. Not your type Willi. Big breasts and stunning legs! I bring her stockings, she lets me put them on. A pack of Sobranie, she'll agree to anything. I need an early finish.

Frisch takes a packet of cigarettes from his pocket, offers it to Hebbel

Hebbel looks in pack

Hebbel takes small hard-covered log book out of breast pocket. Opens it

Hebbel	I'm ready.

Picasso starts in a new place

Picasso	Anthropoid with Satyr - 1912.
Hebbel	20 by 40.
Picasso	Gouache wash.
Frisch	I'll log it. Price?
Picasso	Four thousand francs. Clown and his Mate. Oil on varnished wood.
Hebbel	I'll log AND measure.

Hebbel measures and logs it

Picasso	Shredded Paper. Collage.
Hebbel	Mine. (*Talks as he writes*) 60 by 104.

Picasso pulls out painting

Picasso	Despotic Woman in Trunks. Gouache. 1929.

Picasso slams it back

Hebbel	Sorry? What price was Shredded Paper?
Picasso	Any you want so long as it's under five thousand.

Hebbel	I never measured Man with Stallion.

Picasso tries to find it

Picasso	Where is it? The Toilet - no. Boy Leading a Horse - no. (*Pulls painting half out*)
Frisch	Can we re-wind?
Picasso	I have already. (*Pulls painting half out*) Where is it?
Hebbel	Do I have a price for Man with Stallion?
Picasso	Take a number, divide it by six, times it by ten, and if it comes to over forty thou' you're on your own. (*Picasso pulls at a painting. It won't budge*) Come out sod you!
Frisch	I'll log the next.
Picasso	Come out you bastard painting. COME OUT! Monsieur Frisch, can you hold these?
Frisch	How?
Picasso	Apart. Like this. So I... can...

Frisch pulls the row of paintings apart on either side of the place Picasso points at

Frisch   (*Under strain*) Like this?

Picasso   More. I'll just... ease... this... out.

Picasso half draws out a frame as Frisch holds paintings apart on either side of the one Picasso is extracting

Picasso   Don't let them squeeze back!

Frisch   They want to.

Picasso   They mustn't! If I can inch this out...

Picasso begins to inch out a very large painting

Frisch   They're a weight...

Hebbel   'Specially for an intellectual like you Willi.

Frisch   The weight of something doesn't change according to how clever a person is. It's as heavy for me as it is for you.

Picasso   Can we concentrate please?

Frisch is straining to hold rows apart

Frisch   Yes... yes. Yes.

Picasso	A little more effort. Dammit they're closing.

Frisch makes superhuman effort to keep paintings upright and apart against weight of row

Hebbel	Can't you take it Willi? Muscles not up to it?
Frisch	I'm on top of this… Nothing to me.
Picasso	Monsieur Hebbel, grab the other side? For the sake of my works and Herr Frisch's health.
Hebbel	D'you need to ask? Here, let the men take over. Hold your own side Willi. I'll get this one sorted.

Hebbel takes one side of gap from Frisch and pulls whole row to the right. Frisch is pulling his section of the row to the left

Picasso tries to extricate painting

Picasso	Damn thing won't budge.

Clenched teeth from Frisch as both Frisch and Hebbel try to keep their respective paintings away from the painting Picasso is pulling out. It's like a tug-o'-war

Picasso still 'tries' to pull out his huge painting

Picasso   Monsieur Frisch, would you mind? Can I use your back? To get a better grip?

Frisch   Yes. I... can... take it...

Picasso   Foot up like so. Pull up, like so...

We see Picasso try to climb up on to Frisch's shoulders. The air is full of Frisch's groans and cries

Picasso ends up straddling Frisch's back rodeo-style

Picasso   You can take my weight?

Frisch   (*Trembling voice*) Of course.

Picasso   You won't fall?

Frisch   No...

Hebbel   Keep those legs straight.

Frisch   I will.

Picasso   Hold firm!

We see Frisch begin to buckle under the pressure of holding the row of paintings and supporting Picasso

Picasso seems to be taking his time

Frisch	Could you... hurry? The weight's...
Picasso	Gently does it...
Frisch	Have you got it?
Picasso	I've got it.
Hebbel	Willi, your face. Talk about red.
Frisch	Shut up.
Hebbel	You're not going to explode on us? Bits of Frischy-flesh all over the paintings.
Picasso	It's coming... yes... yes...
Frisch	...Hurry up...
Picasso	Don't wobble!
Frisch	Not... wob'...
Picasso	Nearly there...
Frisch	...'ble ...must ...not ...wobaaaargh...

Frisch crumbles to the floor

Picasso   Got you aaaargh…

Picasso falls on top of Frisch. The whole framework of paintings comes crashing onto floor

Hebbel   Willi! My Christ, you've brought the lot down.

Hebbel crashes to floor under pile of paintings

Picasso   Two seconds! Two measly seconds and she was out. We were that close… Herr Frisch? Where are you?

Hebbel crawls out from pile, sits nursing bruised knee

Hebbel   Only smashed my sodding knee.

Picasso clears frames away

Picasso   DON'T MOVE. GET BACK.

Hebbel   What did I do?

Picasso   Keep away! From my paintings. You may tread on them.

Hebbel   Is that Willi under there?

Picasso clears paintings. Groans from somewhere under the pile, locates Frisch

Picasso　　　(*Feels pulse*) He's got a pulse.

Hebbel　　　Still alive then.

Picasso　　　Wake up. Come back to us.

More groans from Frisch

Hebbel　　　(*Whisper, confidential*) Plan's working a treat.

Picasso　　　So far. (*Quiet voice*)

Hebbel　　　(*To Frisch*) WAKE UP I SAID!

Hebbel slaps Frisch round face

Frisch　　　Wha... what happened?

Picasso　　　I'm afraid you fell. With me on your back. It's all my fault.

Hebbel　　　Lucky Herr Picasso didn't break his neck.

Frisch　　　(*Groaning*) Oh, my head.

Hebbel	You've wrecked the paintings - what you did.
Picasso	I don't like to think how much damage has been done.
Frisch	My head. My shoulder. Aagh...
Hebbel	Is this how you treat great artists Willi? How can you let monsieur Picasso stand on your back if you're not strong enough? Didn't you think what would happen?
Frisch	(*Looking round vault*) God in heaven.
Hebbel	(*To Picasso*) You should've got on MY shoulders. I'm stronger than him.
Picasso	Look at the tear in this work. It's destroyed. And yes... yes... I thought so. It was reserved for the Deputy Ambassador of the American Embassy.

Picasso shows a painting with a tear in it

Frisch	It's not in the middle. Can it be mended?
Hebbel	What with - sticky plaster? (*Laughs*)

Picasso	(*To Frisch*) Did you do this on purpose? ...To teach me a lesson.
Frisch	I promise you, on my word of honour, it was a complete accident.
Hebbel	You're in big trouble when Kimmert gets to hear you've damaged Herr Picasso's paintings. I wouldn't want to be in your shoes.
Frisch	It's you as well. It's not just me.
Hebbel	I never collapsed in a heap just when I shouldn't have.
Picasso	(*Indicating paintings*) Look at them. Like they've been chucked around by a maniac.
Frisch	(*To Picasso*) What can I do? Just say. I'll work night and day to put it right but just tell me what I can do.
Picasso	You can't repair rips. Not in canvas.
Frisch	Can I find a... a restorer? They can work miracles. I'll pay.
Hebbel	Bit late for that.

Frisch	It's a fresh tear, it can be put right.
Hebbel	I think we should ask Herr Picasso what he wants, don't you? He's the one who's had his painting wrecked.
Picasso	There's one thing you can do. That I'd really like. Finish with this. Now. Before you damage anything else.
Hebbel	Get out from under your feet eh. Least that way we won't be bothering you, will we monsieur?
Picasso	No you won't.
Hebbel	Is that alright then? You won't be put out if we just up and piss off leaving this mess?
Picasso	On the contrary I'll take it as a considerate action.
Hebbel	I'm prepared to do as you wish. Your offer of a job-lot price for works not yet seen - that's a generous and a fair offer and I'm accepting. On the grounds it's what officer Kimmert wants. Further it's the decent thing to do after the damage we've caused. How's the wrist by the way?

Picasso	(*Groans*) Gone again.
Hebbel	So, we're at one on our future course of action. (*To Frisch*) Anything to say Willi?
Frisch	I can't think of anything but that rip. I won't feel right till I know it's mended...
Hebbel	Good. Work scheduled for tomorrow is officially on but actually off. I declare tomorrow a free day.
Frisch	No no... we can't do that Franz, especially now with the paintings like this.
Hebbel	Now listen to me, just listen. You're going to do what everyone else does for a change and skive!
Frisch	Look I'm sorry but I'm not... happy. We can't...
Hebbel	I think I can in this case.
Frisch	I'll decide what I do. If we finish today I'm reporting for work tomorrow.
Hebbel	Willi, you absolute pain in the arse.

Frisch	I'm not lying to Kimmert. I've seen too many people come unstuck.
Hebbel	...Think what you could do. All the galleries you could visit...
Frisch	In public? When I'm supposed to be working?
Hebbel	Alright then... spend the day with me. Therese'll find you a friend.
Frisch	I'm not cheating a day off.
Hebbel	This is your last chance. Are you taking tomorrow off?
Frisch	Not if it's not official.
Hebbel	That's it! You've blown it! You had your chance and you've blown it! I'm telling officer Kimmert you solicited goods from Monsieur Picasso in a manner unworthy of a German officer.
Frisch	I did what? What goods?
Hebbel	(*Picking up circus painting*) This painting to be exact.

Frisch	I never solicited that painting. I refused it.
Hebbel	Deny it as much as you like - I know it, and so does Monsieur. I'm reporting you for unprofessional conduct.
Frisch	Monsieur Picasso, tell him this is nonsense.
Hebbel	Monsieur won't fall in with your little games.
Frisch	I'm afraid you've got Monsieur wrong. Please tell him, monsieur.
Hebbel	Deny it as much as you like.
Frisch	I don't give that for what you say Franz. Tell as many dirty lies as you want. Invent them. I've got a witness. An honest witness. (*To Picasso*) Please.

Picasso says nothing, pretending he's looking at his ripped painting

Hebbel	You haggled with Herr Picasso taking advantage of your position, and forced him to accept the pathetic sum of two thousand francs which wouldn't buy a half-decent meal in a bad restaurant.

Frisch	I did nothing of the kind. That's not true.
Hebbel	...And when he told you it wasn't for sale, you said you'd take it anyway and he'd better think twice before he said anything because we were the new rulers of Paris.
Frisch	(*To Hebbel*) I can't believe even you would stoop so low. (*To Picasso*) Can you put a stop to this nonsense monsieur?

Picasso again pretends his attention is elsewhere

Frisch	Tell him what happened? Monsieur Picasso, will you? Herr Picasso?
Picasso	I'm afraid I can't.
Frisch	You can't...? Why not?

Picasso busies himself with arranging paintings, says nothing

Frisch	If he lies about me, you surely won't back him?
Picasso	I want to go home. To rest. Come back refreshed, put my paintings in order.
Hebbel	So now you know Willi. You've got no support.

Frisch	Herr Picasso I'm asking you again. Tell Franz he's talking nonsense and you'll have nothing to do with it.
Picasso	I can't get involved.
Frisch	Please. You can. As a fellow artist if you like. I refused your painting. It was hard but I did. Can't you just confirm that?
Picasso	You need to sort it out between you.
Frisch	(*To Picasso*) I admire you. You're like a god to me. You have a gift... above ordinary men. A wonderful gift. You can't do this.
Picasso	I have to tell the truth.
Frisch	But what Franz says is not the truth and you know it.
Picasso	I've nothing to add.
Frisch	Are you saying if I act like an honest soldier and tell my superior the truth, you'll tell lies about me?
Picasso	I'm saying what I'm saying and I mean what I say.

Hebbel	So Willi... are you going to have the day off, or am I going to drop you in it? Because drop you in it I will, won't I monsieur?
Picasso	I think you're capable.
Hebbel	And Monsieur will back me. If I do.
Frisch	You... you...
Hebbel	Is that a yes?
Frisch	Yes.
Hebbel	You'll do what I want?
Frisch	I'll do what you want.
Hebbel	And not a word to Kimmert?
Frisch	Not a word.
Hebbel	Well that's good. That's sensible. Now we can all relax.
Frisch	I don't see what you get out of this Franz.
Hebbel	If you had any decent bloody social life you would.

Frisch	You have, of course, thought about if we get caught?
Hebbel	How many times do I have to tell you - it's what Kimmert wants. If you'd been less focused on yourself and more on other things you'd've seen that. He won't mind if we take two days and come up with a job-lot price. He won't be checking because he's in the plot.
Frisch	I hate being made to lie. I'm no good at it.
Hebbel	Well shut up and let me do it for you.
Frisch	(*To Picasso*) ...I see great artists aren't always great men.
Picasso	And soldiers who think their hands are clean often find their feet are dirty. Now, please, I've clearing up to do. (*Picasso picks up paintings*)
Frisch	Monsieur Picasso...
Picasso	I have to get on.
Hebbel	Of course you do. At least I know when I'm in the way. To be clear then. The individual

	items we've logged plus three thousand francs the rest. Apprentice works and...?
Picasso	Juvenilia.
Hebbel	That's the word.
Frisch	I didn't pressure you for that painting.
Picasso	Um?
Frisch	It's important... you say it. All my life I've tried to be honest. A great artist has to be honest too.
Picasso	Are you lecturing me?
Frisch	Can't you just say what happened?
Picasso	Let me tell you about honesty shall I? As I see it. Imagine a situation... umm... an army conquers a country. That'll do. They conquer a country and declare all jewellers are to have their stocks listed. Soldiers are detailed to carry it out. Some are not too honest - they filch a ring here and a bracelet there. Some are very honest, they list every item, and never take a thing. These 'honest' ones expect everyone else to be honest too. Their fellow soldiers should take nothing

for themselves. The jewellers should declare every last pin and trinket. But pardon me, isn't it easier for the soldier to be honest than the jeweller? As long as the soldier carries out his orders what does he have to fear? Nothing so far as I can see. In fact he may get promoted if he does a good job. His is the honesty of the oppressor. Is this the same for the jeweller? If he declares all his stock - like the 'honest' soldier thinks he should - could he not be setting himself up for a grab? The authorities would know exactly what he had, if they decided to take it, if - in their opinion - their need was greater, if their war effort required it. So by being 'honest' the jeweller could be allowing, no encouraging, dishonesty in the invading army. He can't take that chance. He decides to lie, say he's got less than he has. This is the honesty of the oppressed. To finish I have this to say - you can't be honest if the work you do has a dishonest basis. So Monsieur Frisch please don't talk to me about honesty as if it's the same for everyone. It rarely is.

Hebbel gives Picasso a round of applause

Hebbel   Get out of that, Willi.

Frisch	…I need to think about it.
Picasso	It will repay some thought.
Hebbel	Admit it, he's wiped the floor with you.
Frisch	You know... I could almost think you two planned this. While I was out the back. About Herr Picasso knowing Kimmert. About me wanting that painting...
Hebbel	I could plot all that? In five minutes? With Herr Picasso? You're giving me more credit than you usually do.
Frisch	It's a thought in my mind.
Hebbel	Well... even if we did - which we didn't - it's the same to you - you're caught. You take a wrong step, you'll burn. Be warned.

Frisch reflects, then turns to Picasso

Frisch	I hope we can meet again. When the war is over.
Picasso	Goodbye monsieur Frisch.

Frisch	I think I know more about artists than I did an hour ago.
Picasso	I think I know more about German soldiers.
Frisch	Well. Goodbye.

Frisch turns and makes his way out to the corridor. We hear his footsteps getting fainter

Hebbel puts his log-book in his pocket

Hebbel	Phew. It worked.
Picasso	You'd better stay lively, in case he...
Hebbel	Don't worry, I'll keep my eye on Herr Frisch alright.
Picasso	Well... enjoy your day with Thérèse.
Hebbel	Heaven calls. Oh... one thing. 'S been bothering me a while now. Do you know Kimmert?
Picasso	Why d'you ask?
Hebbel	Lavender cologne. I never told you he used it.

Picasso	I think you did.
Hebbel	I one hundred per cent did not.
Picasso	Where could I have got that from?
Hebbel	You know him don't you? Come on, you can tell me - we're friends.
Picasso	I can't for the life of me remember.
Hebbel	I'm sure.
Picasso	My memory's gone.
Hebbel	You wouldn't think of dropping me in it, would you, Herr Picasso? I've put myself on the line here. I'd be up shit creek without a paddle if Kimmert were to hear about it.
Picasso	If I'm left in peace I won't cause trouble...
Hebbel	I'll say goodbye then. (*He picks up his overcoat, shakes Picasso's hand, begins to walk towards door. Stops*) ...Word to the wise. I've put my career on the line here. I've left my flanks exposed. Open to attack. I think you know Kimmert. I hope I've done what Kimmert wants. But what if I'm wrong... if I've done what YOU want and

	what I want. If that's the case, and Kimmert were to find out, the shit would hit the fan. If the shit hits the fan...?
Picasso	Watch out for flying shit.
Hebbel	...If I take my crystal ball and gaze into the future what do I see? I see that it might just suit you - if there was ever a problem about what we've done today - to put the blame on me. To say I suggested the job-lot price, when we know who suggested it - and in the name of Officer Kimmert too. Who knows, you might even call on Frisch as a witness to back you up.
Picasso	I'd never do that. You've got my word.
Hebbel	Good. Because if you were thinking along those lines, remember this. Kimmert isn't the only officer in Paris interested in art. There are others, who may not be so friendly to you. Who only love the art of the new order. Who'd like nothing better than to make an example of the work of a degenerate-Bolshevik artist such as yourself. As a warning to others. And the better known the artist, the more they'd like it. So, if you do ever think about dropping me in it...

Picasso	I sincerely hope this is the first and last time my works are ever listed.
Hebbel	A mouth tight shut's the best thing these days.
Picasso	I'll keep my mouth very tight shut.
Hebbel	(*Suddenly smiles, relaxes*) You know I admire you. You remind me of me in many ways. Apart from the art.
Picasso	That's a compliment.
Hebbel	That painting... the circus. You might find someone more grateful than Frisch.
Picasso	Really?
Hebbel	...I've always liked circuses.
Picasso	You?
Hebbel	Since I was that high. They're magic to me. Exotic. A different world. I'll love that painting. It'll have a good life.
Picasso	Now... where was it? (*He rummages*) Here? No. (*Rummages more*) Here? Uh huh. This

	could take hours. Look, give me your details. When I find it, I'll get it to you...
Hebbel	I tell you what. I'll give you a ring. Say a week? And when I buy it you can give me a receipt. To make it legal.
Picasso	A receipt makes it legal.
Hebbel	At two thousand francs. Well... nice meeting you. I definitely think we're a bit the same. A week then.

Hebbel gives Picasso a look. Makes his way out of the vault. We hear his echoing footsteps

Picasso pushes paintings out of way. They make a racket. He lights a cigarette

Picasso inhales, exhales

Picasso	What a pair! Not Frisch so much - a sensitive soul - though I'd trust him as far as I could throw him. Hebbel...! Acts thicker than he is. A cunning sod. (*Drags on cigarette*) Interested in protecting my works. Hah! Interested in nicking it more like! Creep down here one night and have them away! Flog 'em for the war effort. Hang 'em on a wall for Goering to shit to.

Rummages a bit aimlessly through the paintings, stacking some

> What a mess! A complete pig's ear! Mm... maybe leave it. For today. Yes... maybe better.

A painting smacks down on top of another

> Avoid anything they can quote you on. His words. Go for the job-lot if you can. His idea. Herr Kimmert, puppet-master. The man in charge. Let's hope he stays faithful to his love of art, gives us breathing-space, protects us from the vandals. Have I done enough to protect me from the vandals? Does he like my work enough to protect it? (*Looks around him*) They could burn this lot to ashes in an hour. Then say it was an accident.

Our last view of Picasso, as the lights dim, is on him gazing round protectively at his paintings

A last painting smacks down on top of another

> Artful. What I've got to be. As artful as them... As artful as sin.

Picasso threads through mass of fallen paintings to iron door
He exits storage area, swings door shut, locks it

We hear him walk away

THE END